Pack and tick!

Written by Emily Hooton

Illustrated by Claudio Cerri

Collins

Kim picks socks.

Pack and tick!

socks

Kim packs a cap.

Pop it on top. Tick!

5

Kim picks a top.

6

Pack it in. Tick!

- ☑ socks
- ☑ cap
- ☑ top

Kim can pop on the socks.

Kim can dip.

Dad is in.

Kim can pop on top!

Kim sits in!

/c/

14

ck

k

15

🐾 Review: After reading 🐾

Use your assessment from hearing the children read to choose any GPCs, words or tricky words that need additional practice.

Read 1: Decoding

- Reread page 6 and ask: What sort of top is it? (*a T-shirt*) Reread page 12 and ask: What "top" is this? (e.g. *the top of a tower*)
- Go back through the book and take turns to point to and read a word containing /c/. Ask the children to point to the letter or letters that make the /c/ sound (*c, k and ck*).
- Model reading a page slowly, without sounding out and blending. Ask the children to join in and read with you.
- Look at the "I spy sounds" pages (14–15). Say: I can see lots of things that have the /c/ sound. Point to the cat and say "cat", emphasising the /c/ sound. Ask the children to find other things that contain the /c/ sound. (*castle, crown, cake, cup, case, cap, crocodile*) Do the same for ck. (*sock, bucket, flapjack, stick, backpack*) Finally do the same for 'k'. (*king, kick, Kim, key*).

Read 2: Prosody

- Return to pages 12 and 13.
  - Can the children point to the exclamation marks? Model reading page 12 with excitement.
  - Ask the children to read page 13 with a similar feeling of excitement.

Read 3: Comprehension

- Ask the children what they would pack if they were going to the beach.
- Turn to page 3. Discuss the list in the illustration.
  - Ask: Have you ever had a list of things to take or pack?
  - Ask: Why are they ticking the socks? (*Kim has packed the socks.*)
- Ask the children questions and reread the text if necessary to find the answer.
  - On pages 2 and 3: What did Kim pack? (*socks*)
  - On page 4: What does she pack? (*a cap*)
  - On pages 10 and 11: Who is in the sea with Kim? (*Dad*)
- Look together at pages 14 and 15. Talk about the different activities the children in the picture are doing. Ask: What would you like to do, if you were there?